150

Dad Jokes

The Terribly Good Gift

Book for Dads

What did daddy spider say to the baby spider?

You spend too much time on the web!

What do you call the father that you walk all over?

Stepfather

Why did the cookie cry?

Because his dad was a wafer so long!

What did the dad tomato say to the baby tomato?

Catch up!

Why was the baby strawberry upset?

Because his dad was in a jam!

Why don't some fathers have a mid-life crisis?

Because they're stuck in adolescence.

How do fathers suddenly get in good shape on the beach?

By sucking in their stomachs as hard as they can!

What do you call your dad if he freezes?

POPsicle

What do you call someone with no body and no nose?

Nobody knows!

What is the least spoken language in the world?

Sign language!

Why can't you hear a pterodactyl go to the bathroom?

Because the pee is silent!

What does a vegetarian zombie eat?

GRRRAAAAAIIIINNNNS

If you see a robbery take place at an Apple store, what does that make you?

An iWitness

Why can't you trust atoms?

Because they make up everything!

What do you get if you combine Fed-Ex and UPS?

Fed-Up

Why did the invisible man turn down the job offer?

He couldn't see himself doing it!

What has two butts and kills people?

An assassin

What did the pirate say on his 80th birthday?

Aye matey!

What do you call a bunny with fleas?

Bugs Bunny

Why is it nice to live in Switzerland?

I don't know but I've heard the flag is a big plus!

Where does the Easter Bunny like to eat breakfast?

IHOP

What did the rabbits do after their wedding?

They went on a bunnymoon!

What do you call a rabbit that tells good jokes?

A funny bunny

What happened when the Easter Bunny met the rabbit of his dreams?

They lived hoppily ever after!

What kind of jewelry does the Easter Bunny wear?

14 carrot gold!

How does the Easter Bunny stay fit?

Egg-xercise!

Why shouldn't you tell an Easter Egg a joke?

Because it might crack up!

What do you call a forgetful rabbit?

A hare-brain!

How does the Easter Bunny travel?

By hare plane!

Where does the Easter Bunny get his eggs?

From an egg plant!

What do you call a dog that can do magic?

A Labracadabrador

What did the chocolate say to the ice cream?

You're sweet!

Why couldn't the bike stand up by itself?

It was two tired!

What do you call a deer with no eyes?

No idea!

What time did the man go to the dentist?

At tooth hurt-y.

What's Forrest Gump's password?

1forrest1

Why did you lose your job at the calendar shop?

Because I took a few days off.

What did the termite say when he walked into the bar?

Is the bar tender here?

How many tickles does it take to make an octopus laugh?

Ten-tickles

What did the buffalo say to his son when he dropped him off?

Bi-son

Why don't crabs share their food?

Because they're shellfish!

What is Beethoven's favorite fruit?

A ba-na-na-na

Where did the college-aged vampire like to shop?

Forever 21

What did the horse say after it tripped?

I can't giddyup!

What's the loudest pet you can get?

A trumpet

Why wasn't the woman happy with the velcro she bought?

It was a rip-off!

What noise does a 747 make when it bounces?

Boeing, Boeing, Boeing

What do you call a factory that sells passable products?

Satisfactory

Did you hear about the circus fire?

It was in-tents!

Why was the bunny in such a bad mood?

He was having a bad hare day.

Why aren't you familiar with the alphabet?

I don't know why!

What do you get when you cross a snowman with a vampire?

Frostbite!

What does an angry pepper do?

It gets jalapeño your face!

Want to hear a joke about a piece of paper?

But I'll warn you, it's tear-able!

Why do chicken coops only have two doors?

Because if they had four, they would be chicken sedans!

You heard of that new band 923MB?

They're good but they haven't got a gig yet!

Did you hear about the guy who invented Lifesavers?

They say he made a mint!

What do you call a lonely cheese?

Provolone

How do you make a Kleenex dance?

Put a little boogie in it!

What do prisoners use to call each other?

Cell phones

Where does Christmas come before Easter?

In the dictionary!

What do you call an egg from outer space?

An egg-stra terrestrial!

Why didn't the vampire attack Taylor Swift?

She had bad blood!

What did one flame say to the other on Valentine's Day?

We're a perfect match!

What did one magnet say to the other?

I find you very attractive!

Why do melons have to get married in a church?

So that they cantaloupe!

Why are people always tired in April?

Because they just finished a March!

What position do leprechauns play on a baseball team?

Shortstop

Why do leprechauns make such good secretaries?

They're great at shorthand!

Why are leprechauns so hard to get along with?

Because they're very short tempered!

Who is the Easter Bunny's favourite movie actor?

Rabbit De Niro

What do you call leprechauns who collect cans and plastic?

Wee-cyclers!

What do leprechauns love to barbecue?

Short ribs

Why do leprechauns like to recycle?

So they can stay green!

What do farmers give their wives on Valentine's Day?

Hogs and kisses

What treat do dads like for Father's Day?

POPsicles

What did the golfer dad want for Father's Day?

A tee shirt

Why did the daddy cat want to go bowling on Father's Day?

He was an alley cat.

What did Daddy pig put on his Father's Day pancakes?

Hog cabin syrup

What did the panda give his daddy on Father's Day?

A bear hug

How did the panda open his Father's Day card?

With his bear hands!

What do hermit crabs do on Father's Day?

They shellabrate their dads.

What can you give a dad for Father's Day that he'll love and costs nothing at all?

A long nap!

What do you get when you cross a rabbit's foot with poison ivy?

A rash of good luck!

What sport are eggs good at?

Running!

What did the banana's daddy get for Father's Day?

Slippers

What do dads like to snack on for Father's Day?

POPcorn

How do dads like their steak on Father's Day?

On a plate

Why did the broken firecracker get a gift?

It's nice to give Duds gifts on Futher's Day.

Where does Father's Day come before St. Patrick's Day?

In the dictionary!

Why did Dad want to go fishing on Father's Day?

He was hooked on it!

What should you never give a daddy dentist on Father's Day?

A plaque

Why did the kids give their dad a blanket for Father's Day?

Because he was the coolest dad!

Why do dads who like golf get extra pairs of socks for Father's Day?

Just in case they finally get a hole in one.

What did Chewbacca get from his kids on Father's Day?

A plate of chocolate chip Wookiees.

How did the piglet wake his papa up on Father's Day?

With hogs and kisses!

Why was the father so creepy on Father's Day?

He was a daddy long legs!

What did the papa egg say to the baby egg?

You're eggstra special!

What's the last thing the balloon said to his dad on Father's Day?

POP!

Why did the boy give his golf-loving dad a pair of pants for Father's Day?

In case he finally got a hole-in-one!

What did the angler dad want to play on Father's Day?

Go Fish!

What did the dad tomato say to the baby tomato?

Catch up!

What's the easiest kind of flower to find for dad on Father's Day?

Daddylions

What did the ferret do with his dad on Father's Day?

Played POP goes the weasel!

What do dads like to eat for breakfast on Father's Day?

POP tarts

How do dads look on Father's Day?

With their eyes!

What's a fun Father's Day gift for a dad who loves golf?

Silly putty

Why wasn't one Father's Day gift any better than the other?

It was a tie.

What kind of music did the kids play for their dad on Father's Day?

Pop music

Do dads have fun on Father's Day?

a PARENTly

Where do dads like to dance on Father's Day?

Golf clubs!

What's the first thing a dad does on Father's Day?

He wakes up!

What's a good Father's Day gift for an athletic dad?

Speed stick dadoderant!

Why did Luke Skywalker refuse to fight Darth Vader?

It was Father's Day!

Why shouldn't you argue with dad on Father's Day?

Because Father Knows Best.

Why didn't dad get a Father's Day gift on time?

It was chocoLATE!

What do dads not want to be on Father's Day?

Lawnmowers

Did you hear about the restaurant on the moon?

Great food, no atmosphere.

How many apples grow on a tree?

All of them!

Want to hear a joke about paper?

Never mind it's tearable.

Did you watch that program about beavers?

It was the best dam program I've ever seen!

Why did the coffee file a police report?

It got mugged!

How does a penguin build its house?

Igloos it together!

What do you call a Mexican who has lost his car?

Carlos

Why did the scarecrow win an award?

Because he was outstanding in his field!

Why don't skeletons ever go trick or treating?

Because they have no body to go with!

What do you call an elephant that doesn't matter?

An irrelephant!

Want to hear a joke about construction?

I'm still working on it.

What do you call cheese that isn't yours?

Nacho Cheese

Why couldn't the bicycle stand up by itself?

It was two tired!

What did the grape do when he got stepped on?

He let out a little wine.

What is the most ground-breaking invention?

The shovel

Why shouldn't you buy anything with Velcro?

Because it's a total rip-off!

What do you call a man with a rubber toe?

Roberto

What do you call a fat psychic?

A four-chin teller.

What do call a mac 'n' cheese that gets all up in your face?

Too close for comfort food!

You're American when you go into the bathroom, and you're American when you come out, but do you know what you are while you're in there?

European

What's brown and sticky?

A stick

What's the difference between a poorly dressed man on a tricycle and a well-dressed man on a bicycle?

Attire

Did you hear the rumor about butter?

Well, I'm not going to spread it!

Why do you never see elephants hiding in trees?

Because they're so good at it!

What's orange and sounds like a parrot?

A carrot!

Why did the old man fall in the well?

Because he couldn't see that well!

How do you make a Kleenex dance?

Put some boogie in it!

What's the difference between a numerator and a denominator?

A short line!

Father: Let me see your report card.

Son: I don't have it.

Father: Why not?

Son: My friend just borrowed it. He wants to scare his parents.

A little boy asked his father,
"Daddy, how much does it cost to
get married?"

Father replied, "I don't know son,
I'm still paying."

Man: How old is your father?
Child: As old as me.
Man: How it is possible?
Child: He became a father only
when i was born.

"Dad, are bugs good to eat?" asked the boy.

"Let's not talk about such things at the dinner table, son," his father replied.

After dinner the father inquired, "Now, son, what did you want to ask me?"

"Oh, nothing," the boy said. "There was a bug in your soup, but now it's gone."

Jake: What does your father do for a living?

Matt: He's a magician. He performs tricks, like sawing people in half.

Jake: Do you have any brothers or sisters?

Matt: Yep, four half-sisters and a half-brother

A Message From the Publisher

Hello! My name is Hayden and I am the owner of Hayden Fox Publishing, the publishing house that brought you this title.

My hope is that you enjoyed this book and had some fun and laughs on every page. If you did, please think about leaving a review for us on Amazon or wherever you purchased this book. It may only take a moment, but it really does mean the world for small businesses like mine.

Our mission is to create premium content for children that will help them build confidence, grow their imaginations, get away from screens, spend more quality time with family, and have lots of fun and laughs doing it. Without you, however, this would not be possible, so we sincerely thank you for your purchase and for supporting our company mission.
~ Hayden

For more, visit our Amazon store at:

Amazon.com/author/haydenfox